PUBLIC SPEAKING KEYS:

Learning Public Speaking Ways

Alfredo Wiggins

Table of Contents

Introduction

If the prospect of standing up in front of a group of people — a huge or small crowd, online or in-person — makes you sweat, you could suffer from glossophobia or a fear of public speaking.

Presentation skills are a terrific talent I feel most individuals should learn, however. Whether you want to make a profession out of it or simply want to be able to feel comfortable speaking publicly on a personal level.

Regardless of the anxieties, you may have right now, it is feasible for you to become a great motivational public speaker.

What is glossophobia? It is an anxiety condition which goes beyond merely being apprehensive or thinking about being in front of an audience.

You could feel your heart beating and find it difficult to breathe. You might feel hot, disoriented, or sick. You can be shaking uncontrollably or perhaps want to rush out of the place.

Many individuals learn how to overcome glossophobia by attending public speaking training.

Understanding the power of positive thought may also help you conquer your fear of public speaking.

Whether you have glossophobia or are simply apprehensive about your speech, the correct tools can give you the confidence you need to fulfill your public speaking objectives.

Most of us — even those at the top — suffer from public-speaking fear. When I ask my customers what makes them scared, typically they react with the same answers:

"I don't enjoy being watched."

"I don't enjoy the eyes on me."

“I don’t enjoy being in the spotlight.”

And it follows that when they come up to talk, virtually all of them first avoid establishing eye contact with members of the audience. Therein lies the problem: While avoiding direct eye contact may seem like an excellent method for managing speaking anxiety, it makes you even more uncomfortable.

To understand why we need to go far back to ancient times when people saw eyes monitoring us as an existential danger. Those eyes were certainly predators. People were scared of being devoured alive. In reaction to that archaic reality, the amygdala, the region of our brain that helps us respond to danger, swung into full gear. And when our fight-or-flight reaction is aroused, we rightly experience great tension and worry. What does this have to do with public speaking? Turns out, everything.

Here's the bad news: Our brains have translated that primordial anxiety of being observed onto public speaking. In other words, public-speaking nervousness is in our DNA. We view public speaking as an assault. We biologically detect an audience as a scary predator and mount a corresponding reaction. Many people's bodily reactions when speaking reflect how their body might respond to physical signals of danger (shortness of breath, redness of the face, shivering) (shortness of breath, redness of the face, shaking).

So now when we speak in front of a group and feel the eyes watching us, we feel obvious, like a caveman exposed in daylight. And since our brain is telling us that we are under assault, we do whatever is required to defend ourselves. We erect barriers between ourselves and the source of danger — in this example, the audience — to resist the onslaught and dull any risk.

What do these walls look like? We concentrate on our slides. We gaze down. We escape within

our notebooks. In the process, we dismiss the individuals in front of us, wishing them into obscurity. Even the most confident speakers find methods to remove themselves from their audience. It's simply how we're designed.
Speaking in public is no simple undertaking, particularly for individuals who aren't aware of the complexities of public speaking. Often, professionals must communicate with a wide audience, which needs an awareness of both the people listening and the matter at hand. Good speakers realize that they need to communicate in a manner in which the audience can take in the words that they are saying, and which appeals to the crowd in more ways than one.

Good presenters, then, acquire and exhibit specific attributes and personality traits that set them apart from substandard speakers. What are these qualities? And, even if you're not a speaker, why should you also cultivate them? How might these notions enable you to harness your potential and become more successful?

Chapter 1

It's not just you

“There are two sorts of presenters - those who feel anxious and those who are liars.”

Which kind are you? Glossophobia, the dread of public speaking, is considered number one among all phobias, even higher than the fear of death or spiders. Three out of every four persons (75 percent) are impacted. And in today’s job, when public speaking is frequently necessary, that’s a problem.

Considered a social anxiety condition, glossophobia is characterized by the dread of freezing up in front of an audience, of being judged, missing a word, or saying anything that may result in shame. Many individuals avoid speaking in front of others at all costs.

Research reveals that effective presenting abilities are closely connected to success in the job. Thankfully, support is ready today to overcome your fear and create confidence. Check your local resources for training sessions and conferences offered by trade associations or national organizations. For those wanting one-on-one therapy, try visiting a therapist who can teach strategies from Cognitive Behavioral Therapy.

Now this portion, nevertheless, is oriented towards those of you who have a phobia of public speaking or performing or wish to merely build your confidence in this area. It is also pertinent to all individuals who need a confidence boost in general. We may all adjust the following to our requirements. Now public speaking or performing is something that makes many a stomach churn with nervousness.

I'm no exception to this phobia - however, I don't want to be buried alive either. Even in front of a group of friends or colleagues, the prospect of stepping up and presenting fills me with fear.

When I'm ready to speak, I make sure that I consult my team, my mentor, my friends and - critically - the event organiser. This implies that I can get the audience on my side by customizing what I say to them, even if it's just a throwaway joke or a remark on whatever is in the news that day. I also make sure I can gather feedback from the audience to evaluate after the event, so I can utilize it to be better for the next event. This means that when I step up in front of the crowd it's not so much about me and how afraid I am, it's about everyone who has fed in thus far and how far I've come already.

I don't believe I'll ever find public speaking fully comfortable. I simply don't believe I have that type of personality. But I do feel that going through the process has helped me improve and contributed something to the message I'm trying to get through about leadership. After all - as I've come to know - who better to deliver a discussion on strong, confident leadership than someone who is scared by the mere concept of it? Who, indeed!

By being visible, there's also the opportunity of showing someone in the crowd, who could be similar to you, that they can do it too.

On stage

The most essential thing to remember when on stage is to be you, and don't compare yourself to the way other people behave themselves. My presenting style is minimal but considered. Perhaps you're high energy and full of jokes. Any style is excellent as long as it delivers the audience what they came for, has some heart and effort, and is genuine. You'll make it hard for yourself if you strive to be somebody you're not. A few more points:

"The most important thing to remember while on stage is to be you, and don't compare yourself to the way other people conduct themselves."

Never say, ‘I have x points I’d like to make without notes. It’s a sure fire method of forgetting what you had in mind after the first point.

If you’re not aiming what you’re saying toward other panelists, gaze to the back of the room with your head up and shift it about. One of the most typical blunders in public speaking is when the speaker identifies one person who’s listening and concentrates on them. Don’t locate that person because your eyes will unwittingly keep drifting back to them, culminating in an uncomfortable staring competition that makes the rest of the audience feel left out.

Don’t use large terms, talk to the audience as though they are 12 years old. If you start using difficult language people stop listening to what you’re saying because their minds are attempting to decode the meaning of the words themselves. And say everything incredibly slowly, considerably slower than what seems normal in your thoughts. Speaking fast risks losing the audience and holds a host of opportunity for excessive use of filler phrases and words.

Use your hands if you want, it conveys the weight and is another way of expressing meaning.

Finally, smile, and try to enjoy it. No reasonable person is sitting there judging you, and we've all got to start someplace. Practice makes perfect!

Preparation

Don't accept an offer to public speak unless you've had time for a good several hours of preparation beforehand. Ideally, spaced across a few days. Your responsibility is to provide the audience with as much fascinating and valuable information as possible. By sauntering on stage with a few lines of notes scrawled down on the tube journey, you're insulting the audience and they'll despise you for it. It's not about you, it's about what you know.

"Don't accept an offer to public speak unless you've had time for a good several hours of preparation beforehand. Your responsibility is to provide the audience as much fascinating and valuable information as possible."

There's an approach in feature writing that's called 'imagine your Pookah'. The Pookah is your ordinary audience member. How old are they? At what point in their career? What do they care about? What three questions would your Pookah want to be answered? Whether you're appearing on a panel, chairing it, or giving a keynote, the above applies. Put yourself in the Pookah's shoes, then work out what you're going to tell them. Structure is crucial too. Don't start with your greatest stuff, reserve it for the middle as you ease the audience in with something that sets the atmosphere like an overview, quick history lesson or figures relevant to the topic in hand. Then, offer your brain a storyline to follow as a narrative does with a beginning, middle and finish. Some things to consider:

How much time have you got? If you're presenting on a panel with three other individuals that lasts an hour, you need to prepare enough content that takes up fifteen minutes. A keynote is all yours. If you're chairing a panel, you need enough questions to keep the debate going until time is up. Prepare, then practice out loud and time yourself at least three times. Ideally, find a critical buddy to offer you input. I recall better if I write everything I'm going to say on paper after I've written the last edit. It's an exhausting chore, but one that leads in a smoother flow of dialogue on stage since I'm not reading from a piece of paper the entire time.

Unless you're making a major speech, you won't need to know everything you're going to say by heart. It's a debate thus talk will flow. However, rehearsing exactly what you're going to say in the first two minutes will make you feel confident and relaxed having started on a good foot. You'll need to introduce yourself so think of a few things you're proud of career-wise to share (which shows you know what you're talking about). For notes, Wenham uses a stack of A5 cards that she writes a headline on, followed by three main points, with the subject of the next card on the bottom right to stay ahead of herself.

On a panel, if you're not the moderator, the person that is should get in touch with you to discuss what you're going to talk about, and how that ties into what the other speakers have to say. That will guarantee there's no overlap and will help drive your own preparation. Something to recommend if the moderator doesn't take the initiative themself.

There's no escaping feeling apprehensive, but there are actions you can do to make sure it doesn't overwhelm you. This method worked for me: Go and locate a peaceful area beforehand where you may spend 10 minutes to mentally prepare. Take 10 deep breaths, in through your nose and out through your mouth, reducing any tightness in your shoulders and jaw at the same time. Then rehearse what you're going to say out loud in those first two minutes a few times, carefully. If your inner monologue begins being nasty, override it with positive statements instead; it's okay, this is going to be fine, you've done tons of prep, you know what you're talking about.

"There's no escaping feeling scared, but there are actions you can do to make sure it doesn't overwhelm you."

It's only you who understands you're going to climb a metaphorical mountain, the audience are simply come to hear some valuable information before moving on with their lives. Speaking of which, I find it helps to have something to look forward to at the end. Knowing that whatever happens, life goes on, seems to alleviate some pressure.

Chapter 2

Before you start, have faith

Confidence is one of the most potent skills in public speaking. Here's why you must believe in yourself 100 percent, so others will do the same.

Faith is vital to success. If you don't have FAITH in yourself; BELIEF it will work out in THE END, then you can only have doubt and if you DOUBT you can accomplish the life you deserve, odds are you won't.

Faith doesn't imply everything will be wonderful ALL THE TIME. As a human being, you are promised hardships and bad times. Having FAITH implies you BELIEVE that in the end, if I keep going if I keep seeking solutions if I continue to do WHATEVER IT TAKES to achieve, I WILL SUCCEED!

Having an unshakable conviction in YOURSELF is vital to a successful life.

Most of us just do not believe in ourselves enough. And that's why we lack the self-confidence to let our views be heard loudly and clearly.

Chapter 3

Consider the worst case scenario

Having the capacity to visualize the worst potential situation of your public speaking, which you may identify as an imaging exercise, is a terrific method to investigate what you are frightened of.

Experiencing anxiety at the prospect of having to speak in public, as is the case with other sorts of phobic anxieties as well, typically, comes because you are envisioning a certain situation. Often, we don't grasp what stays behind our thought of terror, and we could fail to contemplate the fact that the awful plots we envisage, are not too realistic.

Here is what a worst-case imagined situation may look like:

I am on a platform and should begin to speak any minute now, but when I turn to the crowd, all I see are cold, hostile, judging looks, expecting to analyze everything I say and do, to find flaws. I start to talk, and then I realize I can't do it. My voice is too wobbly, and I stammer, I am a sweaty, frightened mess that cannot control her body, so everyone can see what's happening. To calm down, I explain that I just need a minute and get a glass of water. Some people in the crowd start to chuckle, while others are leaving the room. I'm trying to continue, but I can't. All I prepared for my speech has mysteriously evaporated, leaving my mind blank. The only thing I can think about is how I'm going to collapse, ashamed and afraid. Finally, it becomes impossible to endure the situation longer, and I decide to declare to everyone that I have to leave, then hurry toward the door and walk out, feeling like the greatest coward in the world.

Although terrible conditions may undoubtedly arise, it is quite improbable that they would be this awful, that you would leave amid your speech, or that individuals from the audience would be this harsh and judgemental. However, even if you haven't started your worst-case scenario, your attitude can be that you tried, failed, and should never subject yourself to such suffering again. Asking yourself, "What is the worst that may happen?", and coming up with a similar scenario to the one mentioned above might help you recognize that practically, it is probably impossible for your darkest fears to become true, which can have a very relaxing and powerful impact.

Reality Is Not as Catastrophic

If you picture the worst conceivable event and live it out in your mind, you'll likely be better prepared for the actual one, which wouldn't be as disastrous as what you imagined. Besides, analyzing your biggest fear will help you come up with ideas and plans of what you can do, in case reality throws an impediment your way.
everything that can go wrong, will go wrong.' This appears to be particularly true when you consider public speaking.

Speaking in front of people is already a daunting experience, and when things start to go wrong during the presentation, it can become much more stressful. The good news is, that if you're aware of and prepared to manage certain setbacks, you can simply recover.

You run out of time.

Dragging a presentation on longer than your permitted time is one of the most typical blunders made by newbies in public speaking.

It's vital to attempt to remain inside your given time. If you can, finish a little sooner than you're meant to! Remember, your presentation time is an unspoken contract with your audience. Professionals, today a day are highly time-sensitive. Having a presentation run longer than it's meant to might lead your audience to grow upset with you, while a shorter presentation will likely cause them to be satisfied with you.

Unfortunately, occasionally some presenters go, over their permitted time and might cause your time slot to be reduced, you should still endeavor to complete in your provided time window.

You lose your line of thinking.

Have you ever wondered why you lose your train of thought? You understood precisely what you were talking about and you even knew what you were going to say, and suddenly, poof! Your thoughts went blank, and you're left standing about looking perplexed.

Even the finest public speakers may occasionally draw a blank. The difference between an experienced speaker and a novice speaker is that an experienced speaker understands what to do when this circumstance happens.

Losing your train of thought may be disconcerting, and lead you to feel like a deer caught in the headlights. Luckily there are several strategies to recover that when done correctly, may make it look like you never lost your train of thought, to begin with!

Chapter 4

Getting an audience interested in what you have to say

There are certain steps involved in the preparation of a good speech. The first step is to choose and narrow a topic. If one is not provided a specified subject, then one must establish a working topic to direct the presentation. At other times when you are given a subject, it is not out of place to restate or restrict the scope of the supplied topic if it helps you manage the presentation properly. The next step is to comprehend the aim of the speech.

This is the politics underlying public speaking. A speaker should know for sure what s/he sets out to accomplish and the anticipated result from the audience. Sometimes, presenters intentionally try to bamboozle their audiences merely to win such individuals to themselves. The speaker should next collect resources for the speech. Even if it is an extemporaneous delivery, the speaker should still take a time to think through his/her ideas in his/her thoughts. This should be followed by drafting an outline and then writing the speech if it is one to be read.

A variety of approaches have also been found in public speaking. There is the spontaneous approach which entails making a speech on the spur of the moment — without preparation previously. The speaker gets to depend on his/her expertise, experience, and oratory skill. Even when you have barely a minute to deliver an impromptu speech, nevertheless spend around 10 seconds to get yourself synchronized. A memorized speech is composed, committed to memory, and given without reading it out. It requires a good oracy skill on the part of the speaker. There is also the extemporaneous speech when the speaker is expected to have an outline to guide the presentation without needing to remember or read verbatim from a script.

Some guidelines are crucial for a public speaker to flourish in the creative act. First among them is the necessity to be oneself, both in attitude and speaking mannerisms. Traces of mimicry of someone else's way of communicating might win a speaker disfavor. Appearance is another element a speaker needs to be cautious of since it tells volumes about him/her. A speaker must also maintain eye contact with the audience at random intervals to acquire information about their attention and interest. Importantly, too, a speaker should gesticulate throughout a presentation. This forestalls boredom.

How do you get an audience interested in what you have to say and keep them engaged? How can you connect to the audience in a manner that enables them to relate to you and comprehend your story?

To be a successful speaker, these are the five attributes that are necessary.

Confidence: Confidence is crucial when it comes to public speaking. Being confident in your delivery will help you to be viewed as an authority in your field. Your audience will be more inclined to trust you and consequently, trust the stuff that you are putting out there. Confidence makes you credible, knowledgeable, and believable. To properly display confidence, you have to be confident enough to be yourself throughout your presentation. If you can be yourself in front of an audience, they are going to be more likely to feel like they can connect with you. If you attempt to behave differently than you typically do, you may come across as fake, and the audience will be less likely to feel connected to you or your knowledge.

Passion: Why would an audience want to hear about your tale if you don't appear excited about it? Let your audience know why you do what you do. Why do you enjoy what you do and why do you wish to spread your message? If an audience can see and feel your enthusiasm, they will be more interested in hearing what you have to say.

Ability to be succinct: Even if you're one of the most entertaining and engaging public speakers, it's crucial to keep your presentation brief and to the point. The attention span of your audience isn't lengthy. You have to catch their attention immediately and hold their attention by going through your presentation easily and efficiently. If your presentation is longer than twenty minutes, you may want to consider dividing the presentation into smaller portions. Each part might be a bit different or entail audience involvement so that you are keeping them on their feet.

Ability to tell a story: A presentation is more successful and interesting when it doesn't feel like a presentation. Know how to communicate your narrative to your audience. Give them the context for all of the information you are sharing. Rather than merely presenting statistics and formal bits of information, share your experiences and the tales that have led you to where you are. If it isn't your narrative, share other stories or experiences from history or others that you know. Stories help individuals recall more information since they are more engaged with your presentation.

Audience awareness: Make sure before heading into your presentation that you know the audience that you're speaking to. You should know who they are and what they do. By understanding this knowledge, you'll be better able to connect to them and deliver to them in a manner that you believe they would react to and learn from best.

Demonstrating these skills as a public speaker may make or break a presentation. When designing a presentation, think about what you would react to. Think about whether you would be passionate about and interested in your presentation and the information you're presenting. To be a good speaker, you have to be willing to step out of the box to connect, relate to, and engage with your audience. Make sure your narrative is one that your audience will want to hear and will remember long after the presentation is finished.

Chapter 5

Conclusion/Overcoming public speaking fears

Tips for overcoming your speaking nervousness

- Be confident in your subject: The better you understand your topic and the more enthusiastic you are about it, the less likely you'll make a mistake or go off course. Take some time to ponder what questions the audience may ask and have your replies ready.

- Know your audience: Reference something everyone in the audience will relate to. Maybe everyone is suffering from the hot, humid weather. Use the similarity as an icebreaker.
- Get organized: Carefully arrange the facts you wish to offer using an outline, maybe

color-coded, on a little card. Studies demonstrate that presenters feel comfort in having something in their hand, so integrate visual aids and props into your presentation.

- If possible, visit the venue where you'll be speaking: Get acquainted with the environment and rehearse with the equipment you will be utilizing.

- Avoid reading word for word: Practice your whole presentation numerous times. Start by reading it. Progress to utilizing solely the bulleted talking points you have written on your little card. By practicing, you'll grow more familiar with the structure of your presentation.

- Challenge particular worries: When you're fearful of something, you may exaggerate the chance of negative things occurring. List your particular anxieties, and then consider alternate good outcomes.

- Make strong eye contact with various persons in the audience: There is comfort in feeling that you are in a discussion with an individual and not conversing “en masse.”

- Don't fear a moment of silence: If you lose sight of what you're saying or start to feel worried and your mind goes blank, it may seem like you've been quiet for an eternity. In actuality, it's probably just a few seconds. Just take a few calm, deep breaths before beginning.

- If you make a mistake, be human: We all make errors. Laugh and move on.
- Relax, knowing that 75 percent of the audience can relate to your worry!

- Visualize your success: Imagine the confidence that will come from the smiles and cheering after you complete. Some presenters claim that towards the conclusion of their presentation, their frightened butterflies have been replaced with a feeling of success.

- Do some deep breathing: This can be very calming. Take two or more deep, slow breaths before you get up to the podium and during your speech.

- Focus on your material, not on your audience: People generally pay attention to fresh information — not how it's delivered. They may not detect your uneasiness. If audience members do sense that you're scared, they may root for you and want your presentation to be a success.

- Get support.: Join a group that assists persons who have problems with public speaking. One excellent resource is Toastmasters, a nonprofit organization with local chapters that focuses on teaching individuals in speaking and leadership abilities.

You're on a journey to persuade hearts and minds of your ambitious plan to alter the world. Don't allow any fear of public speaking to stand in the way of presenting a fascinating tale or inspirational message.

Being apprehensive in public speaking settings might affect how others perceive and respond to your vision. "Almost everyone is apprehensive to some level when it comes to public speaking. " The trick "is to recognize that fear is there for a purpose. Fear is a drive to act."

"Courage is not the absence of fear. Courage is the capacity to stare fear in the face and continue to go ahead... Only by strengthening our bravery will we prevent our anxieties from forming and then keeping us small."

Craft a Powerful Presentation

Once you've collected the bravery to get started, how will you construct a presentation that catches the attention of your audience? How will your ideas come together to produce value and drive change?

It begins by understanding what you're passionate about and articulating that enthusiasm with an authentic voice.

What's important is that you, the true you, speak. That there's no artifice about this. That it's you, taking something you're passionate about, finding the correct tools, and utilizing them to express that message as forcefully as possible.

Finding and sharing your narrative via public speaking may be tough. Usually, when arranging a speaking presentation, you feel you must leave aside your personality qualities — the distinctive phrases you prefer to use, or the hilarious manner in which you tell a tale to a buddy, to make room for a more "professional" or "polished" version of yourself.

We tend to assume that public speaking and sincerity cannot live on the same platform but this is not the case.

Public speaking is not about employing words or information you believe your audience wants to hear. It's about presenting a concept that matters to you and doing it with honesty.

Fear of public speaking is a typical kind of anxiety. It might vary from minor uneasiness to paralyzing dread and terror. Many persons with this anxiety avoid public speaking situations completely, or they suffer through them with trembling hands and a quavering voice. But with preparation and effort, you can conquer your fear.

If you can't conquer your phobia with practice alone, consider obtaining expert assistance.

Cognitive behavioral therapy is a skills-based approach that may be a beneficial treatment for lowering anxiety about public speaking.

As another alternative, your doctor may prescribe a soothing medicine that you take before public speaking. If your doctor recommends medicine, test it before your speaking engagement to see how it affects you.

Nervousness or nervousness in some circumstances is natural, and public speaking is no exception. Known as performance anxiety, additional instances include stage fright, test anxiety, and writer's block. But persons with severe performance anxiety that involves substantial concern in other social contexts may have a social anxiety disorder (sometimes termed social phobia) (also called social phobia). A social anxiety disorder may need cognitive behavioral therapy, medicines, or a combination of the two.

www.ingramcontent.com/pod-product-compliance
Lightning Source LLC
LaVergne TN
LVHW020533160826
845677LV00015B/4035

* 9 7 9 8 8 4 4 3 3 3 6 4 4 *